© Jo Anne Schneider 2016

Acknowledgements

Many thanks to Alexandra Levitt, Scott Fischer, Ken Kalumuck, and Frances, Pat and Kevin Callahan for their comments on earlier drafts of this guide.

© Jo Anne Schneider 2016

Table of Contents

Introduction 1
What is Social Capital? 4
    Connections that lead to resources 5
    Reciprocal, Enforceable Trust 6
    Cultural Cues (cultural capital) 9
Three Different Kinds of Social Capital 15
    Bonding Social Capital 15
    Bridging Social Capital 17
    Linking Social Capital 19
Identifying and Using Social Capital in the Person with Disabilities Networks 21
    Creating a Social Capital List 26
    Using Social Contacts to Access Resources 28
    Following Leads from your Networks 31
    Keeping Track of Contacts 35
Employment Systems for People with Significant Disabilities ... 38
    Changing Legislation and Changing Attitudes 40
    Customized Jobs and Discovery 45
Building New Social Capital 52
    Creating Reciprocity and Long Term Relationships 53
    Building Social Capital to Help Develop Careers 55
    Building Appropriate Cultural Capital 57
Choosing and Working with Organizations 59
    Organizational Social Capital 61
    A Word on Job Clubs 64
    Things to Look for in Choosing an Agency 65
Tips for Effectively Using Social Capital in Employment for People with Disabilities 68

© Jo Anne Schneider 2016

Appendix: The Theory and Research Behind Social Capital ... 72

References 75

Related Publications 77

    In this Series 77

    Other Key Publications by Jo Anne Schneider on Social Capital 77

© **Jo Anne Schneider 2016**

Introduction

David is a young man with moderate intellectual disabilities who graduated from high school and was interested in clerical work. After graduation, his parents asked their friends and family if anyone knew of appropriate work for David. A friend who worked in a large accounting firm said that they were looking for some clerical help and recommended David to the managing partner. David was hired to do copying, filing, and other clerical tasks for the firm. He has worked at the company full time for over 10 years.

Krystal has been blind since birth. She has done well in school and earned a BA in counseling but was unable to find work in her field. Referred to a job club through her vocational rehabilitation counselor, she developed strong networks among other members of the club. They shared leads they had heard – mostly to call centers or packaging jobs. She found that these leads would be for part-time work unrelated to her field. With no other options, Krystal returned to applying for positions on line with few interviews and no offers.

Ryan is a disabled veteran with a traumatic brain injury and loss of part of one leg. He had little work experience and had just finished high school before joining the army. He received some mechanical training while in the military, but felt he could not use these skills due to his disabilities. Instead he thought he would try for a warehouse job. Using contacts through the VA, he attended a veteran's career fair and talked with a number of recruiters about warehouse and

© Jo Anne Schneider 2016

related jobs. While these recruiters were helpful and took applications, these contacts never led to interviews or jobs.

All of these examples show people with disabilities attempting to use connections to find jobs. David's family used traditional mechanisms to find work for him - talking to family and friends. Krystal and Ryan focused on job clubs and career fairs because both had learned through workshops at local job centers that social capital, which they thought meant connections, was the key to finding work. Social capital is often touted by experts as important to find work, build social integration, and generally expand the ability of people with disabilities to become part of the community. But Krystal and Ryan's connections led nowhere while David was successful. That's because Ryan's connections at the job fair really weren't social capital. Krystal's job club connections did not have the right resources to help her find the kind of work she wanted.

Social capital is widely used in policy, workforce development initiatives, human services organizations, and by those interested in building community or civic participation. While the concept has a common definition, it is often not defined by those using it, frequently used to mean several different things, and often misunderstood. This guide is designed to explain in practical terms what social capital means and how people with disabilities can use social capital to find and keep jobs. This guide is meant for people with disabilities and their families, a companion guide is designed for staff at agencies providing employment services for people with disabilities.

The discussion starts by defining social capital and the various ingredients that people need to pay attention to in identifying and using social capital. Next, the guide uses examples to explore social capital through people with disabilities' networks and building new social capital. This section includes a chapter for families of people with moderate to severe intellectual and

© **Jo Anne Schneider 2016**

developmental disabilities (IDD) about finding jobs related to their gifts and interests given the special needs of adults with this kind of disabilities. While this chapter is targeted toward people with IDD and their families, the process of discovery and developing customized jobs could be used for anyone. Another chapter discusses working with employment agencies and their staff, focusing on identifying the social capital available through agencies. A final section summarizes key points in using social capital effectively. While the guide is based on academic research, it does not use academic language or references. Information on the theory behind social capital and key references are in an appendix.

© **Jo Anne Schneider 2016**

What is Social Capital?

Social capital is the social science term for building relationships that help individuals, families and agencies access the resources they need to meet their goals. Social capital is defined as *the social relationships and patterns of reciprocal, enforceable trust that enable people and institutions to gain access to resources like social services, jobs, or government contracts*. Building social capital is a slow process that involves people developing trusting relationships with both other people and organizations. Families and organizations both develop networks of others with similar goals and interests that they exchange information, goods, and services with on a regular basis.

This definition helps us understand why David's connections led to jobs while Ryan's did not. David's connections came through long established relationships among family and friends. The accountant who told David's family about the job had known him for most of his life and understood his skills and abilities. As such, he provided a knowledgeable reference to his company. As a trusted employee, this accountant's HR department took his recommendation seriously and was willing to give David a chance. The enforceable trust of long standing relationships from reliable people made a difference.

Ryan had a referral to the job fair from the VA placement agency, a trusted source that would provide some social capital. But just getting entry into the job fair did not represent established trust with the employers that attended. While they were glad to talk to Ryan, the one-time contacts at the job fair were not enough to bring Ryan's application to the top of the pool given his limited experience. Without an established relationship to the firm through someone the company trusted, VA status was not enough to lead to a job.

© Jo Anne Schneider 2016

While these examples might imply that people should only use their established networks find work, social capital is more subtle than that. Taking a look at the ingredients that make up social capital clarifies how it can best be used to help individuals with disabilities find jobs.

Connections that lead to resources

Everyone has connections, but to function as social capital that connection must lead to needed resources. For example, Mark is a person with developmental disabilities that is part of a large, supportive family and an active member in his family's church. His family and friends through church and other networks have provided lots of resources for Mark over the years like rides to programs, companions, and even funding for special camps. But this large network did not have the resources to help him find a job. Mark is fascinated with birds of prey and dreamed of working at a park, zoo, or animal rescue organization. His family and friends worked primarily in construction or service sector jobs and knew no-one that had anything to do with birds. As a result, they offered Mark lots of jobs helping out at their companies, but nothing related to his interests.

This does not mean that networks must have connections to a particular job or place to provide social capital. If the networks of either individuals or the agencies that serve them know how to foster necessary connections, that also can generate productive social capital. For example, David's family did not have connections themselves to appropriate jobs for him, but they knew how to work through their friends to find employers with openings. Later sections of this guide will discuss other ways to develop connections.

© Jo Anne Schneider 2016

To serve as social capital for employment, those networks need to have access to paying jobs related to those interests. For example, Krystal's job club friends could give her leads for jobs, but not the kind of work she wanted to do. Her vocational rehab counselor also suggested she volunteer to provide counseling through an emergency hotline. While this experience may lead to a job later, the fact that the hotline received pro-bono services from established counselors in the area meant that this experience would not lead to a paying job. However, it could lead to connections with counselors that would have the appropriate social capital to help her in future.

Networks also need to have access to the right hiring managers, not just organizations with jobs. For example, one of Krystal's job club friends found a job in the cafeteria at a hospital. While the hospital did hire counselors, her friend didn't know anyone in the counseling department and had no way to establish the kinds of trust with that department to make an effective referral.

These examples highlight that identifying effective social capital means more than just seeing if your network has connections, but if they have the right connections to find a paying job doing the kind of work the person with a disability wants to do. If not, other mechanisms can be used to build social capital or provide links to resources that will help the person with a disability develop appropriate social capital over time. Ways to do this will be discussed later in this guide.

Reciprocal, Enforceable Trust

Why would someone use their connections to help someone find a job? The answer is a sense of trust and mutual obligation.

© Jo Anne Schneider 2016

The kind of trust that leads to social capital is not generalized trust like trusting your neighbors, the police, or the local government. Its specific trust in an individual, their networks, or the organizations they are associated with. Usually, to effectively generate social capital, those helping someone find a job and the person or organization hiring has an established, reciprocal relationship with each other.

For example, compare the kinds of trust involved in the hiring decisions for David versus the companies at the job fair Ryan attended. David and his family both had established trust with the accountant that helped him find a job. The accountant was trusted at his work place. In both cases, this established trust encouraged the firm to give David a chance.

Ryan benefited from the generalized trust that the companies participating in the job fair had with the VA and the patriotic impulse to hire veterans. He was treated with courtesy by recruiters and allowed to attend the job fair based on this generalized trust. But the reputation of the VA was not enough to lead to a hire for a veteran without related experience.

Trusting relationships can come from organizations, not just individuals. Marion was a bookkeeper who was deaf. After taking off work for several years, she sought help through the local Jewish employment agency's disability unit to find another job. The organization had a strong reputation for reliable employment referrals. They referred her to a company run by someone active in the local Jewish Federation. The agency had a strong relationship with this company through board appointments to the local federation that it belonged to and previous successful hires from the same agency. The enforceable trust between company and agency served as the social capital connection for Marion.

© Jo Anne Schneider 2016

Those organization relationships don't necessarily need to be through people or organizations directly known to each other. The Jewish agency has made other successful referrals to organizations in their community that are part of the Federation network, but had no previous experience with this employment service. Ties between the company and the Federation provided the enforceable trust to encourage the company to give special attention to referrals from an agency that belonged to the Federation. In this case, the social capital came from the wider network, not direct links to this firm.

Established, reciprocal relationships are important because they mean that a relationship will not be damaged based on one bad experience. While the Jewish employment service has a strong reputation, occasionally someone referred does not work out. Companies continue to use this agency as an employment service because they know that most of their participants remain on the job and perform successfully and that if someone doesn't work out, they will be quickly replaced. These established relationships with employers keep employers hiring from the agency and families of people with disabilities using this organization.

This suggests that identifying networks that can effectively find jobs means looking at the strength of the relationships as well as the number and simple availability of connections. Identifying relationships should involve looking both for relationships between organizations that the person with disabilities and their networks are affiliated with as well as individual networks. Employment agencies' trusted networks are a key resource for employment for the individuals they serve.

© Jo Anne Schneider 2016

Cultural Cues (cultural capital)

People use their social capital to help those that they think will represent them well and help them preserve established relationships. This final ingredient in effectively using social capital involves knowing the right ways to behave, speak, dress, etc. to encourage others to help the person with a disability find work or employ them in their company. In social science definitions of social capital, the ability to fit in is called *norms, cultural capital, or cultural cues.* Appropriate cultural cues differ depending on the network, workplace, community, and other factors. Cultural capital is separate from social capital, but it is essential for activating social capital. Besides looking for networks, staff and people with disabilities need to understand the important cultural cues that will enable social capital to be effective.

Cultural capital appears as an important factor in the successful employment stories described earlier. The friend who referred David for the position in the accounting firm came from the same class background as the people working in the firm and knew that David had learned how to dress, speak and handle instructions in a professional workplace from his upbringing. The family friend who made the referral was able to provide additional guidance to David so that he learned to fit in at the workplace. As a bookkeeper with years of experience, Marion knew the general culture of office accounting departments. The Jewish employment agency was able to fill her in on the culture of her new workplace through their previous experience with this company.

© **Jo Anne Schneider 2016**

Problems with cultural capital for individuals can take many forms. In some cases, it is a problem with the way a person presents themselves or the case for employment. For example, Krystal was very shy and still dressed in jeans as she had in college. In job interviews, she wore a plain, gray suit her mother had bought for that purpose. While she was dressed appropriately, the subdued suit and her demeanor meant that she appeared very quiet and soft spoken to interviewers. She talked about her interest in course subject matter, but not interacting with potential clients or helping people address their problems. As such, interviewers thought she did not have the communication skills or strength of personality to succeed as a counselor. In her volunteer positions, she appeared younger than she was due to her clothes and manner.

One of the counselors at her volunteer placement noticed that Krystal was effective with hotline clients and started giving her tips on how to interact with others in a way that showed more confidence and ability to handle a counseling interaction. She also suggested more professional clothes that made Krystal look like a professional. Through slowly developing these social skills, Krystal was able to obtain an internship that was the first step toward a job.

The good news about cultural capital is that it can be learned. Everyone who successfully moves through life learns to fit into a number of different cultural environments. Most of us learn that we dress, behave, and talk differently in different places. For example, talking and dressing one way with friends and another at a workplace or church. Sometimes this is as simple as helping someone like Krystal learn how to dress and act appropriately for a specific job.

© Jo Anne Schneider 2016

At other times, this can be complicated. For example, the worlds of organizations that work with wild birds require specialized training, knowledge, and have their own unique cultures. It is difficult for someone like Mark who learned about birds from books and the internet to learn this culture. The same is true for anyone entering a professional field like counseling or computers. As discussed below, it may be better to identify mentors or people within the person with disability's networks with this knowledge to help them learn the appropriate cultural cues.

In some cases, cultural capital issues are difficult to break through. For example, Mark had family and church networks that were supportive of people with developmental disabilities but had deeply ingrained cultural beliefs that someone like Mark could probably do cleaning and lifting, but not much else. When his employment specialist at a disability employment agency sought to connect him with a wildlife rescue organization and pursue interviews with staff at a state park, his family complained that the agency should instead just "find him a job." Successfully placing Mark involved convincing his family that this slower approach to job placement was worthwhile.

Cultural stereotypes that people with disabilities are not smart enough or capable enough to work present another potential cultural barrier to finding a job even for people with mild disabilities. Many people who a job seeker with a disability might interact with while looking for work - from friends to potential employers and even disability employment agency staff, still think that people with disabilities are only capable of low-level manual labor. Advocates for full employment for people with disabilities often talk about the four Fs (food, filth, flowers, and filing) as the kinds of jobs people with disabilities

© Jo Anne Schneider 2016

have been relegated to for years. This is true even for people with physical or sensory disabilities acquired later in life after they had worked successfully as professionals for years. And people with hidden disabilities (for example, intellectual disabilities, mental illness, people with visual or hearing disabilities with no visible cane or hearing aids) face accusations that they are not really disabled or faking it.

Cultural beliefs about people with disabilities vary from country to country, state, region and even across communities, so a job seeker can't simply assume that others will believe in these stereotypes. But you need to be prepared to address them while looking for jobs and among co-workers and supervisors once you find work. Researchers and experienced practitioners working in employment for people with disabilities assert that while general education campaigns help with negative attitudes about the capabilities of people with disabilities, the best way to convince an employer of an individual's potential as a worker is through connections with experience with people with disabilities and actual experience hiring or working with someone with a disability.

In essence, this means changing the cultural beliefs of those without disabilities that are part of the employment process through building social capital. As discussed later in this guide, if you encounter negative stereotypes, look for someone affiliated with that company who has experience with people with disabilities or people with your kind of disability. They are more likely to use their common connections and knowledge of the culture of the workplace to help you. Or look for ways to volunteer or intern with this company to show them first hand what you can do.

© **Jo Anne Schneider 2016**

In other cases, culture is ingrained in hiring practices. Take for example Selma, a blind woman with a graduate degree in human resources and significant experience in providing professional development and trainings on working with people with disabilities. Selma's vocational rehabilitation counselor learned of a staff training job in a related government agency where she had many contacts. Selma had all the skills and the appropriate cultural knowledge to do this job well, but she could not meet one hiring criteria in the job description. This agency only hired from within, with an agency culture that people started as vocational rehabilitation specialists and worked their way up to other positions in the agency. The job required that the training specialist have worked as a vocational rehabilitation counselor for 7 years and had managed vocational rehabilitation counselors for 3 years. This requirement was unrelated to any of the actual skills required in the job description and was just meant to keep those who had not come up through the ranks in this agency or a similar one from being hired. Even though she understood the culture of the agency, she could not successfully compete for the position because of this agency requirement. Changing this situation would probably require civil rights complaints against the agency and would be difficult to enforce even if they were successful.

This discussion of the role of cultural capital in effectively using social capital implies that people with disabilities and their supporters need to pay attention both to the nature of the networks and the cultural cues that they need to display in order to convince a connection to facilitate employment. In some cases, this involves simply paying attention and using the right cultural cues. In other cases, appropriate culture needs to be learned by a few words of guidance on dress or particular culture of a job. In other cases, successfully finding a job

© **Jo Anne Schneider 2016**

involves bringing in someone else who is part of a network one is trying to access who can teach appropriate cultural capital and use the cultural cues needed to gain entry to a company or network of those with needed resources.

© Jo Anne Schneider 2016

Three Different Kinds of Social Capital

Social capital researchers identify three types of social capital, bonding, bridging and linking. Bonding social capital involves long established networks of close friends, family, or professional networks of people who are similar and share the same values. Bridging social capital means networks that cross boundaries of culture, region, or some other significant difference, but where everyone in the network are generally equal. Linking social capital involves reciprocal, enforceable trust across power boundaries like an employer and their staff person or an agency and the government entity that funds it. While each kind of social capital works differently, each is equally important in the quest to help people with disabilities find the resources they need to find jobs or fulfill other life goals.

Bonding Social Capital

Bonding social capital networks often involve the people you trust most and can rely on no matter what. For example, friends, family, or the people in a faith community where you have attended for years. These are the people and organizations that both individuals and staff turn to first when seeking any resource because they are most likely to try to help. As with David, family and close friends are more likely to use their networks to help a person with a disability find jobs.

Bonding networks can also be professional or personal networks outside of family and friends. For example, the disability agency that wrote the job description only hiring from within that agency or similar ones was practicing bonding social capital by making it difficult for outsiders to get hired. Hobbies like model railroading, dog breeding, or bird watching can develop bonding

© **Jo Anne Schneider 2016**

networks. Or they can include people from a particular region, ethnic, or religious group.

The important thing about bonding social capital is that people share the same culture and that it is difficult for outsiders to get in or use the network's resources. Bonding networks are often safe, for example, Krystal's job club or the VA service center and VFW post where Ryan spends much of his time. But this safe environment is a closed environment, and means that the individual may not be integrated into the rest of the community.

Bonding networks may offer limited resources because of the closed nature of the network. For example, Mark's network had lots of resources to find him a job cleaning, shelving or providing other physical labor, but nothing to help him find work that met his interests. Given that everyone in the network worked in blue collar or service sector jobs, the culture of the network did not support trying something different. In order to help Mark meet his goals, he would need to look outside these networks.

Bonding networks can either be a supportive environment that will help people succeed or have limited vision of people's capabilities. Sometimes they are both. For example, Krystal's family and friends supported her desire to complete college and become a counselor. They provided a range of assistance and encouragement for her to meet her goals, but did not have the networks to help her find a job. Mark's networks did not support his goals, making it necessary for disability agency staff to step in and support finding a job that reflected his interests.

Bonding networks are important resources for employment development, but they may have their limits. While it is important to identify social capital resources in these networks

© Jo Anne Schneider 2016

for people with disabilities, they may not be sufficient. Identifying and developing bridging and linking social capital is equally important for people with disabilities and the people that aid them.

Bridging Social Capital

Bridging social capital involves reciprocal, trusting relationships developed across group boundaries. For example, Martin, diagnosed with high functioning Autism at an early age, came from a family of architects and engineers. Martin developed an early interest in the natural world, which became a focus on plant biology in high school. While Martin's bonding networks of family and their friends knew little about plant biology, they knew how to help him develop networks with those interests due to their own educational backgrounds. Relying on the guidance of teachers and the biologist at a local nature center, Martin's family enrolled him in nature camps as a child and clubs related to his interests in high school. The nature center biologist provided volunteer opportunities and used her networks to find him an internship during college. These clubs, teachers and the nature center biologist introduced him to networks with similar standing and education as his family, but in a different field.

Through participation in clubs, camps, volunteering, and internships, Martin developed trusting relationships in his intended field over time. These relationships were reciprocal because Martin contributed through his activities and gradually became part of the network of people interested in plant biology in the area. His encyclopedic knowledge of plant species was highly valued in the group.

© Jo Anne Schneider 2016

Bridging social capital does not develop over a one-time connection between people with no other social capital connections. The two people need to develop a basis for trust and reciprocity first. This is the reason that going to a one day job shadowing event, a common early employment strategy for people with disabilities, does not lead to jobs. The person with a disability may meet people doing similar work, but has no mechanism to develop a relationship with that person.

These examples highlight two important aspects of bridging social capital. First, bridging connections usually come through a bridging individual or joining an organization related to the network the person wants to join. The teachers and nature center employee that helped Martin are one good example of bridging individuals. The established counselor volunteering at the hotline with Krystal is another. Through developing these relationships, a whole world of connections opened up into their chosen careers.

Second, using bridging social capital involves learning the cultural capital important in the new network. Part of the clubs, camps and volunteer experiences Martin engaged in involved learning what plant biologists actually do on a job and the culture of these workplaces. The same was true with Krystal in her volunteer position. Particularly for someone like Krystal who is shy, developing appropriate cultural cues is essential for getting a job.

As with cultural capital, bridging social capital can be built for individuals. Ways to build social capital will be discussed below. It is important to remember that the goal is to develop lasting reciprocal relationships across boundaries. This involves both

© Jo Anne Schneider 2016

developing connections and learning the appropriate cultural cues to interact appropriately in the new network.

Linking Social Capital

Like bridging social capital, linking social capital involves crossing boundaries, but the person or organization receiving support from the network usually has less power than the one providing the connection. For example, an established professional serving as a mentor for a person with a disability who wants to enter that profession. We can see many examples of linking social capital in the examples in this guide.

The teachers and established professionals that helped Martin are one example. Agency contacts, like the Jewish employment agency networks that helped Marion find work are another. In this case, the counselor used linking networks related to the Federation to encourage the company to interview Marion.

As with bridging social capital, linking relationships are established over time. For this reason, the employers at the job fair did not take extra steps to help Ryan. While the VA is a known agency, no VA employment counselor with an established relationship with these companies pursued the contact. Instead Ryan tried to develop an employer relationship on his own through an interview at a job fair. Without a strong linking or bridging relationship between the employer and the VA, employers were not willing to extend the trust associated with linking social capital to Ryan.

While the person receiving advice and links to jobs is in an unequal relationship to the person providing social capital access, linking social capital is still a reciprocal relationship.

© **Jo Anne Schneider 2016**

Martin, Krystal, and others that receive internships or successful job leads provide benefits to that profession and organization through their quality work.

The recipients of linking social capital also contribute to the network by referring other good candidates to their employers. Once established in their careers, they help build and expand the network by serving as linking social capital to others. These actions also develop reciprocal, enforceable trust within the linking network.

As with bridging social capital, successfully using linking social capital involves using the appropriate cultural cues expected by the linking network. No-one is going to refer someone for a job or internship if they don't dress appropriately, know the basic language of the profession and otherwise look like they will fit in. However, if someone lacks some of the social skills but comes through an established individual or organization, a linking social capital connection may provide the tips on appropriate cultural capital to help the newcomer become a successful employee and member of the network.

© Jo Anne Schneider 2016

Identifying and Using Social Capital in the Person with Disabilities Networks

Job development has always involved making connections for the person looking for a job. Family and friends have often used their social capital to help people with disabilities find work. For example, I once had a skilled tradesman who was deaf work in my home. He shared that he had learned his trade from his father and was working in the same company. On multiple occasions, family members use their connections to find work for a person with a disability. For example, David's family used their bonding social capital through friends to find work for David. David received no employment help from an agency or the state vocational rehabilitation agency (Voc Rehab).

In my earlier work with low income job seekers, in study after study, more than half found their jobs through personal networks. Personal networks also play a prominent role in finding people with disabilities work. For this reason, employment specialists, job developers and other disability services agency staff involved in helping people with disabilities find work are encouraged to identify personal networks for the people they serve and them to help with locating jobs. Individuals and families turning to Voc Rehab or a disabilities employment agency for help can expect questions about your networks. This is part of their job.

As a first step in finding work, a person with a disability needs to identify their own networks and those of their families or other significant supporters to identify people who can help find work. This chapter shows how to identify and access those networks step by step.

© Jo Anne Schneider 2016

Identifying social capital consists of the person with a disability and their family or *circle of care* naming the people in their network, listing their relationship to the person with a disability, and listing ways this person could help the person reach their goals. A *circle of care* is a group of people interested in a person's future that have convened to help them find work. For people with IDD, *circles of care* may be mandated by state policy and may include the members of a person's family, staff from agency's providing employment services, their guardian (if they have one), and friends or interested members of their community like a former teacher or mentor from their church. The individual identifies the people to be involved in the *circle of care*, often with the help of staff or key family members. While *circles of care* are an increasingly common strategy for people with IDD and other significant disabilities, developing a small group of friends, counselors, mentors and professionals is an excellent strategy for anyone looking for work.

Simply listing connections is not identifying social capital. Remember that social capital networks have access to needed resources and are willing to put those connections to work for the person with the disability. Simply identifying someone in the person's personal network in that field might not meet these criteria. For example, while Mark's social and church networks did not include anyone who worked with wild birds, a relative did work as a grounds keeper in a wild life refuge. But this person had no connections to the skilled professionals that worked directly with birds.

For this reason, identifying networks needs to involve asking three questions:

© **Jo Anne Schneider 2016**

1. Does anyone in the individual's personal networks either work in the field where s/he has an interest or work in a place that is related to that interest?
2. Does that person have useful connections to places or people that could lead to a paying job related to that interest?
3. Is that person willing to use those connections to help the person with a disability find work in that field?

These questions need to be answered for anyone identified as part of the individual with a disability's social network. If the answer is yes, asking the network connection to mentor the person with disabilities to help them learn the cultural cues and behavior they will need to succeed would be the next step. Mentors can serve as the bridging link into that network as well as help identify ways interests can translate into a viable job.

If those contacts don't exist, people can build networks through a series of mechanisms. This will be discussed later in the guide.

The first step in using social capital to find work is to clarify the person with disabilities' interests and potential jobs. This can be done by working with an agency, vocational rehabilitation, or someone who does occupational therapy to assess interests, capabilities, and possible options. Identifying professional resources will be discussed in more detail later in this guide.

Regardless of whether or not you work with a professional, it is helpful to brainstorm interests, strengths and weaknesses for the individual with their family or others who know them well. It is important to determine what the individual wants him or herself, not what the family or friends think would be a good job. Either by or him or herself or with family, answer the

© Jo Anne Schneider 2016

following questions. The answers should be written down and then compiled into a list of potential jobs or attributes of work and work places.

1. What are the person with disability's interests? Are there activities or topics that s/he finds fascinating? What does s/he like to do?
2. What are this person's gifts? What kinds of things does s/he do really well?
3. What are this person's weaknesses? Are there things s/he can't do? For example, activities that involve fine motor skills or multiple tasks. Can s/he do these tasks if they have assistive technology or other supports?
4. Are there activities or jobs that the person does well, but really doesn't like doing? For example, a person may be a neatness freak and do a great job of cleaning and organizing, but have no interest in jobs that would involve cleaning or organizing.
5. What kind of environment does the person need to do well? Do they like the outdoors? Do they need a quiet environment or a job that involves working alone? Do they like busy places?
6. What kinds of supports does s/he need to do well? Once they learn a task, do they need continued support?

These questions are the first step in job *discovery*, a process used to help develop a job related to interests and gifts for person with significant disabilities. *Discovery* and *Customized jobs* will be discussed in more detail in the next chapter.

In developing these lists, it is important to focus realistically on current interests. For example, Kevin is a young adult on the autism spectrum with problems with fine motor skills. He is very social and can learn tasks with some repetition and someone breaking them down into parts. When he was younger, he was fascinated by birds and still can identify birds from around the world instantly through a picture or hearing their call. But he is no longer interested in them and when asked said he didn't want to work with birds. He currently is fascinated with music, playing by ear and with an encyclopedic knowledge of a wide range of music.

In developing an interest and career profile, Kevin and his family focused on music. Kevin has a high school diploma and is capable of talking to people about music and stocking CDs or other forms of music. With limited functional math ability, he is unable to run a cash register or do anything that would involve math. He does not do well in environments with too much noise or confusion, but would do well in an environment where he could talk with people and hear music. Given this profile, he expressed interest in working in a music store or a larger store that sold music.

Often, it is best to focus simply on a job that involves an interest rather than a particular job. For example, Kevin could stock shelves and help customers pick out music in a store, but could not be a generalized store clerk. Developing *customized* jobs that use a person with disabilities' interest is an important strategy when looking for jobs. Customized jobs fill a need in a business but are created specially to use the gifts that the person with a disability offers. For example, Kevin could work in a music archive helping people pick out music from particular artists or genres.

Once the interest and abilities profile is created, think about the kinds of places that might have use for someone with those

© **Jo Anne Schneider 2016**

interests. It is often helpful to look for small businesses as they are often more open to creating an opportunity for a person with a disability. Make a list of potential places that might be appropriate for that person to work. But remain open to other ideas. Once you start talking with people that know more about those interests, many new ideas and places to consider will appear.

Creating a Social Capital List

The next step is to make a list of relevant contacts. Start with your family and close friends. Is there anyone in those networks that knows something about the topic or work in a company that could use someone with those interests? Make a list of these people, including their names, what they do, how they know the person with a disability, and contact information.

Making these kinds of lists is sometimes easier with people with a specific profession or job in mind. For instance, making a list of counselors for Krystal, book keepers for Marion, or HR professionals for Selma is a pretty easy task to understand. If someone says they really want to stock shelves in a store, that person may have a lot of people who work in stores that could help.

But it's important to think beyond just people doing that same job, although those in the same field is the best place to start. For example, counseling is performed in a wide array of settings, from schools, to nonprofits offering a wide array of services, to private practices. Book keepers and shelvers are needed in many types of companies. Look for people who would have connections to the staff in these fields at their workplaces or places where they volunteer. For instance, a school teacher might be able to connect Krystal to a friend in the counseling

© Jo Anne Schneider 2016

staff at their school. A mid-level manager in a furniture company could refer Marion to their accounting department.

When developing these lists, think broadly about people or organizations that might be able to help. For instance, the music director at the family church might be able to help someone with an interest in music like Kevin find work. If the person with a disability is interested in becoming a book keeper, is there a coach or parent from Special Olympics that works in that field or works in the finance or book keeping department of a company? As with Martin, is there someone at a nature center s/he frequents who can guide an interest in biology?

Krystal and Mark's stories show that these potential contacts need to have access to people actually working in the fields of interest. For example, as with Krystal's friend who worked as a cook in a hospital or Mark's relative who worked as a grounds keeper, people in different jobs in a large company may not have connections to professionals related to the person's interests. You need to determine if these people really have access to anyone who can help when adding them to your social capital list.

It is also important to determine if that person is likely to help the person with a disability find work. Remember that Mark's friends and family did not think that he could do anything but cleaning and other manual labor. Even if they did work in a field that involved wild birds, they would be unlikely to help.

This kind of creative thinking can help a job seeker get out of a rut of going to job fairs, applying for jobs online, or going to job clubs with no results. Let's take Ryan for an example. Thinking about his networks, he remembered that a neighbor of his parents that he'd known for years worked in a warehouse. Asking around his local VFW post, he found several retired

© Jo Anne Schneider 2016

warehouse workers who still had contacts with their former workplaces. These contacts formed the start of his social capital list.

Often, it is helpful to create a worksheet in excel or a similar program to keep track of contacts. These lists can then be used to record results of contacts and new contacts. Here is one example of a list for a young adult named Peter with developmental disabilities that wants to work with animals:

Name	Occupation and where they work	How do you know them?	Willing to help?
David R	Works at a Petsmart	friend from school	yes
Mary M	Volunteers at an animal shelter	Grandmother's friend	yes
Dr. Jones	Veterinarian	family vet	maybe, likes Peter
Marsha L	Dog groomer	Special Olympics parent	yes
John D	Works at dog walking service	Church member	No, called P retarded
Rachel L	Activity director at nursing home with pets program	Church member	yes
Chris P	Works at independent pet store	Neighbor	maybe

Using Social Contacts to Access Resources

Once you have created your list, it is time to use it to find jobs. You will want to contact everyone on your list who you think would help. For example, Peter and his family would want to contact everyone on the list above except John D. Depending on how things go, it may also be worth talking with John to determine if he might be willing to help. Sometimes people who seem disinterested or unsupportive can change or at least are willing to provide some information.

It is helpful to start with people you know best and trust first. For example, David and Rachel, who know Peter very well, might be the first people to contact for an information interview. The goal of these interviews is NOT to ask if they have a job for Peter, in fact that question should not be asked until the very

© Jo Anne Schneider 2016

end of a conversation. The goal is to learn about the workplace and kind of tasks or jobs available in that workplace.

For example, David might be asked what it is like to work at Petsmart, the kinds of things that staff do, if there are any tasks that are often left undone or anything that could be done to make the work easier, and last, who to talk to at the Petsmart about learning more about that store. Rachel might be asked about the pets program, where it is located, and who to talk to at the agency. Peter and his family might also ask if there is any way Peter could visit when the program is going on to get to know the staff or if he could help out when they come.

For someone with a specific job in mind, these conversations can be more targeted. For example, Ryan might ask his friends who worked in warehouses about the various jobs available there, what kinds of skills they need, what the work is like and what it pays. He may ask if they can connect them to someone responsible for supervising or hiring in the parts of the warehouse where he wants to work. He might also ask if the friend would be willing to talk to his contacts at the warehouse to facilitate his contact with that company.

It's also important to remember that social capital involves established relationships. For example, Kevin's mother asked a nearby used book store about opportunities for Kevin when shopping there and was instructed to talk to the owner. On another shopping trip, she met the owner who said that they don't have the time or space in the crowded bookstore to work with anyone like Kevin, but the staff person she spoke with first encouraged the family to bring him by.

A little later, Kevin's father went shopping for music with him at this store. Kevin knocked some things over, but talked knowledgably about music. It is unclear what impression he left

© Jo Anne Schneider 2016

with the store staff. Without regular interactions with the store and an established relationship, it does not appear that this contact could lead to a job.

With someone that knows the person really well, the last part of the conversation might be focused on potential jobs. For example, David's family talked to their friends about David's skills with filing and other office work, asking if they knew of any place that might be able to use his skills. The friend who worked at accounting firm that hired him knew they needed someone with those skills and was able to make the referral.

Empowering people to develop social capital means explaining to them how these networks can help and reinforcing the importance of cultural capital. When talking with your initial contacts, ask the person to identify the cultural cues that are important in that network and explain ways to dress, talk and behave. When working with a person with a disability, emphasize that these cultural elements are as important as connections.

It is helpful to develop a list of questions to ask people in your social network. But these are mostly conversations about the work and the workplaces and need to be kept conversational. The following are a few examples of specific questions:

1. Tell me about what it is like to do this kind of work? Or What is it like to work with pets, music, in a warehouse?
2. What kinds of tasks do people do at this workplace? What is it like to do them?
3. What kinds of different jobs do people do? What are the qualifications to do them? How do people get these jobs? What is that work like? How much does each job pay?

© **Jo Anne Schneider 2016**

4. Are there any tasks that people don't like to do or are often not finished? Could someone with my skills/family member's skills do them?
5. How can I learn more about doing this kind of work?
6. What is your workplace like?
7. Is there someone at your workplace I can speak with to learn more about it and see if there is a way to get involved there?
8. Are there opportunities to help out or volunteer to learn more about this kind of workplace?
9. Who else would you suggest I talk to? Could you talk with them to ask if they would be willing to talk with me?

The last question on this list is very important, because one goal of talking with your social networks is to identify other people who can help that can lead to a job. You may need to talk to a large number of people to find an opportunity for paid work and this may take some time. The first step is to develop contacts and talk to each one about what they know and, ultimately, if they know of potential paid opportunities.

After each conversation, add any contacts to your list and explain who referred you. Strategies for tracking contacts will be discussed later in this chapter. The important thing here is to send a thank you email or note to everyone you talked with. It is equally important to keep up the relationship with your initial contact as those from your closer networks are most likely to help you and suggest other leads over time.

Following Leads from your Networks

Ideally, each person you contact should give you several more leads. Ask them to be sure to give you the best contact information for them and if they would be willing to make an introduction to that person. The key thing here is using an already existing relationship to help you find work. You are

© Jo Anne Schneider 2016

relying on the social capital of the people in your network to expand your network and ultimately find work.

The social capital that your contacts use could be from personal friends or colleagues, or through an organization they are affiliated with. For example, Selma, the HR professional who was blind, contacted a colleague who had moved to another company and had an information interview with her about new opportunities in HR. This individual referred her to a colleague at another company who had an opening that fit Selma's skills.

The counselor from the hotline who became a mentor for Krystal referred her to a company she knew well from her graduate school that hired many alumni. Although the hotline counselor had no personal connections at that agency, she identified herself as an alumni of a school highly respected by that company and used the school's social capital to help Krystal.

Following these leads starts with a brief email, phone call, or personal introduction to make contact with the new source. If the person who referred you does not know of a current appropriate opening, DO NOT contact that person or company asking about jobs. These should be information interviews and clearly identified as such.

For example, the hotline counselor, Maria Black, might introduce Krystal to the director of a domestic violence counseling service at the company in the following way:

> I am an alumni of State University's counseling program and have followed the work of your counseling center's domestic violence program with interest for many years. I have been working with a young woman named Krystal Dean at DV hotline for a year and feel that she has a great future in counseling. Krystal has a BA and is exploring graduate school and looking for work. I am

© Jo Anne Schneider 2016

> writing to introduce you and ask if you would be willing to talk with her about your program and future careers as a counselor? She is also interested in learning about jobs appropriate for someone with a BA degree.

Krystal would then follow up with this person to make an appointment. Her email would attach a resume and look something like this:

> I am writing to follow up on Maria's introduction and ask if I could please schedule some time to learn more about your organization and a career in counseling? I graduated with honors from Davis College and have been volunteering at the DV hotline for over a year. I am interested in continuing to work in the field and would be grateful for your advice. Could you please suggest times and dates that would work for you?

When there is an actual job lead, the person can follow up him or herself with an application or a request to talk further about general openings. For example, Selma might send an application for the opening, starting the letter with a sentence saying: *Marsha Knight suggested that I apply for the position of HR diversity director at your company.*

Selma's friend Marsha could then send a note to her friend at the other company saying that she had referred Selma and talking about her sense that she would do well in that job. While Marsha may not be named as a reference, the colleague at the other company is likely to contact her and rely on that personal relationship to learn about Selma from a trusted source.

Note that none of these requests for meetings mention the person's disabilities. Unless disability is a particular characteristic for a job, this should not be mentioned in an

© **Jo Anne Schneider 2016**

introduction. Instead, highlight your strengths and ability to do the job. The disability may come up later when setting up the meeting or during it, but always highlight your ability to perform with accommodations.

Once you have set up the meeting, do research on the company so that you can ask targeted questions about their work and needs. As with initial conversations with your close friends and family, ask similar questions to those suggested in the last section. Do NOT ask about job openings until the very end if you are not interviewing for a job. Then ask generally about potential openings and the employment process.

Introductions to new contacts may go differently for someone with more severe disabilities like Mark, Kevin, or Peter. For example, Mary, Peter's grandmother's friend, might ask the director of the animal shelter where she volunteers if Peter could come with her and shadow her for a day. In this case, Mary would explain that Peter has developmental disabilities but highlight his experience and interest in animals. Peter would be introduced to the shelter by Mary, meet the staff, get a tour, and be able to show his abilities while helping Mary. He would also learn more about the work there so that he can decide if he really likes it. At the end of the visit, Mary and Peter would ask if he could come again.

You have three goals for all of these information interviews and visits:

1. To learn more about the work and potential openings.

2. To develop relationships with these individuals that can be built on to potentially develop your own social capital relationships with them.

© **Jo Anne Schneider 2016**

3. To ask for more contacts.

By following through on contacts, you will eventually find someone who can tell you about an opening or who may offer you some work once they have learned more about you. Remember, you are either reinforcing the social capital between the person that referred you and their network or developing your own. If these contacts are part of your future career network, hopefully you are doing both. For this reason, it is important to be patient and make sure you look toward continuing a relationship with the person you have met.

Keeping Track of Contacts

It is always important to keep track of contacts you make in looking for a job and identifying new networks. This can be done in excel or a similar program, or just on paper. The chart below is an example of what Peter's experience might be looking for work that involves pets.

© Jo Anne Schneider 2016

Name	Occupation and where they work	How do you know them?	Willing to help?	Results?
David R	Works at a Petsmart	friend from school	yes	Said that there were always lots of openings and would be glad to make an introduction to manager (Wally)
Mary M	Volunteers at an animal shelter	Grandmother's friend	yes	Arranged visit to animal shelter
Dr. Jones	Veterinarian	family vet	maybe, likes Peter	Referred Peter to boarding kennel he works with
Marsha L	Dog groomer	Special Olympics parent	yes	Polite, but no leads
John D	Works at dog walking service	Church member	No, called P retarded	
Rachel L	Activity director at nursing home with pets program	Church member	yes	Referred Peter to nonprofit that ran the pet visiting program
Chris P	Works at independent pet store	Neighbor	maybe	Told Peter and his parents to stop by, meet owner - Karen
Wally D	Manager at Petsmart employing David	referral from David R	?	Showed Peter the pet store, said they have a corporate program to employ people with disabilities and provided contact info. Recommended work through agency
Travis K	Manager animal shelter	referral from Mary	yes	Said Peter could volunteer anytime. Peter started volunteering once a week
Ming Lee	Owner, Happy Farm boarding kennel	referral from Dr. Jones	?	Showed Peter the boarding kennel and said that they often need people to help feed the animals and play with them in the evenings after most staff go home. Peter could visit again and help out
Jenny J	Founder, Pets visiting program	referral from Rachel	?	Responded to a phone call from Peter's mother, explained that they only work with people that could bring their own pets and provide their own transportation plus pay volunteering fees
Karen L	Owner, For Paws pet store	referral from Chris P	?	Explained that this was only herself and her son's friend (Chris) and didn't need any help. But referred to dog washing service
Vishram B	Owner, Dog Wash	referral from Karen L	?	Showed Peter dog washing service and said they could use help cleaning up after dog washing. Said Peter could try it out as a volunteer

This chart shows both the people from Peter's networks that had something to do with pets and the contacts made through these initial contacts. Note that all but one of Peter's initial contacts led to additional referrals. Of those referrals, three led to volunteer opportunities: working at an animal shelter, a boarding kennel and a dog wash. One suggested that he apply for a job through a corporate program and provided information. In most cases, these initial referrals would lead to still more referrals, and the process may take several dozen leads before leading to a job. As an illustration, this possible set of outcomes for Peter shows a much shorter process.

© Jo Anne Schneider 2016

What happens in a case like Peter's? Peter may volunteer at the animal shelter as part of his activities of daily living through a day program for a long time. He may try working at both the dog kennel and dog wash. The dog wash is closer to home and has daytime hours, but he finds that all he is doing is cleaning up and says he does not want to work there. He loves working at the kennel and playing with the dogs. After about a month he is offered paying work there. Given transportation needs, he works there for four hours three times a week. Petsmart eventually offers a position stocking, but he turns it down.

Using social capital to find jobs may take some time, but it ultimately is more likely to lead to positions with the kind of support a person with disabilities needs to find work. And using social networks can be more effective than more traditional methods. Social capital can be used both through personal networks and by working with organizations that provide employment related services to people with disabilities. Working with agencies will be addressed later in this guide. Next, I outline some issues for people with significant disabilities like IDD in the employment process.

© Jo Anne Schneider 2016

Employment Systems for People with Significant Disabilities

This guide is meant for people with a wide range of disabilities and the family members, friends and others in their personal networks who help them find work. The challenges faced by people of average or better intelligence, high school educations or more, and ability to speak like others in their communities who become disabled later in life may be different from those with disabilities from birth or developed in childhood with similar capabilities. Still, the same strategies work to find jobs.

This is also true for people with significant intellectual and/or developmental disabilities like cerebral palsy, autism, downs syndrome, and a host of other disabilities that qualify adults for services from state developmental disabilities agencies and social security income supports. For example, a number of state and federal government staff in professional or managerial positions have cerebral palsy that confines them to a wheelchair and require them to use assistive technology and assistants to speak. There are many highly educated professionals with autism like Temple Grandin, the professor and animal behavior specialist. Many people with IDD who have trouble communicating or only have an educational certificate instead of a high school diploma do hold jobs that use their special gifts and are directly related to their interests. So far, this guide has shared the experiences of Mark, Peter, Kevin, and David, all people with significant IDD served through the IDD services system and eligible for social security.

That said, the process of finding work and the expectations of family members, agency staff and the general public about the possible career paths for people with significant IDD is different

© **Jo Anne Schneider 2016**

than for someone with a physical, hearing, or visual disability, mental health disability, or even someone with significant IDD that is high functioning enough to complete high school or more, communicate, and find work without relying on the state developmental disabilities employment system. As I developed this guide, I heard many family members say, "well this wouldn't work for someone with my child's level of disabilities." Even the families that see their children's gifts and are ready to do everything possible to help them reach their potential know how difficult it is for someone without a high school diploma and who has trouble communicating or acting appropriately in social situations to find meaningful work.

I attended a number of workshops for Maryland's Developmental Disabilities Administrations' *Employment First* initiative that brought in national experts to show how to develop jobs that weren't simply loading groceries, gardening, cleaning floors, or data entry. These experts advocated developing customized jobs through a process of discovering the person with disability's talents and interests, then finding employers that could use those skills. But even at these workshops, staff working hard to implement what they learned acknowledged that doing this work was costly, time consuming, and meant working against all the negative stereotypes of the abilities of people with IDD. And the agencies that sent staff to these workshops knew that many of the other agencies providing employment services still focused on developing work crews that got contracts to do gardening or cleaning or finding the people they served jobs at grocery stores or other large employers as greeters, baggers, stockers, and cleaners.

This chapter provides a brief overview of the recent legislation that is trying to change employment prospects for people with significant disabilities and the ways that state developmental

© **Jo Anne Schneider 2016**

disabilities agencies and private organizations serving people with IDD are implementing these new regulations. The chapter also provides a very brief overview of the process of developing customized jobs in order to help families either find agencies using this process or do it themselves.

All of the people used as examples in this chapter are classified as moderate IDD and have been in special education and adult programs for the disabled throughout their lives. Most have a special certificate of completion from high school for people with disabilities, not a high school diploma. My goal is to give families and people with significant disabilities a basic outline of governing legislation and best practices to help them advocate for their rights and find appropriate agencies to help find jobs the individuals with disabilities want.

Changing Legislation and Changing Attitudes

Society wide views about appropriate employment for people with significant disabilities have changed a lot in the past few decades. There has been a gradual movement away from expectations that people with IDD would either not work at all or perform manual labor in sheltered workshops or on work crews formed by developmental disabilities agencies. Sheltered workshops can range from stuffing envelopes or assembling products to doing customer service or performing data entry in a facility serving only people with disabilities. Work crews usually have a small group of people with disabilities working under a staff person performing cleaning, grounds maintenance, or similar work.

Another common strategy to employ people with disabilities involves disability agencies employing the people they serve in in-house jobs at the agency like clerical jobs or in a print shop or

© Jo Anne Schneider 2016

restaurant at the agency. In house jobs are sometimes a training experience and stepping stone to work in the community. These activities may pay minimum wage or better doing work similar to other businesses, but the people with disabilities still work in a disability agency with other people with disabilities and their staff.

If in house or work crew jobs are a stepping stone to community jobs in a reasonable period of time, they are an important way to help people with significant disabilities acquire skills and experience to compete for jobs in the community. However, in all cases, people with disabilities are segregated from the general population, working only with others with disabilities and sometimes paid less than minimum wage. These jobs do not always lead to integrated jobs in the community.

Initiatives to integrate people with even the most severe disabilities into the community sought by the Independent Living movement, self-advocates, and forward thinking agencies since the 1970s have now become the expected standard for services for people with disabilities. For several decades, the goal of employment services for people with disabilities has been to find a regular paid job, working in the community just like anyone else. Often, typical community jobs fit into the four Fs (food, filth, flowers, filing), like cleaning at a McDonalds or stocking at a grocery store, but they provide a paycheck and mean the person with disabilities is working with people without disabilities and interacting with the general public.

This societal movement toward meaningful community jobs has been reflected in the government services provided to people with IDD. Most of the funding for services for adults with developmental disabilities comes through the Center for Medicaid Services (CMS) and is administered by state developmental disabilities agencies. Since closure of

© Jo Anne Schneider 2016

institutions, services for employment and day programs funded through state IDD agencies have come through the Medicaid waiver for home and community based services (HCBS). Medicaid waiver rules have continued to fund sheltered workshops, work crews and day programs where people with IDD are segregated from others in the community, but has gradually pushed for services that led to "community jobs."

In 2014, federal rules for HCBS changed to focus on integrating people with disabilities into the community in all aspects of their lives. States were given five years to redesign their systems to ensure that all people with disabilities served through Medicaid waiver funding no longer spent their days in disability agency programs, sheltered workshops, or segregated work crews, but were involved in activities in the community. Building on the *employment first* movement, most states also redesigned their day and employment services for people with IDD to focus on trying to find everyone paid work in the community, regardless of the severity of their disability. The new HCBS rules and employment first mean that services for people with disabilities are expected to:

- **Provide all people with IDD or otherwise served through HCBS funds with activities in community settings integrated with people without disabilities.** For example, disability agencies would develop activities in a general community center that include both people with and without disabilities instead of offering a day program in their own facility. Programs only for people with disabilities in separate agencies will only be funded after special review.
- **Ensure that activities reflect the interests of each individual, and not slot people into agency developed general programs and any job the agency can find.**

© Jo Anne Schneider 2016

- **Focus on finding employment in the community as the primary goal for people with disabilities, regardless of the severity or nature of their disability.** Integrated jobs means that sheltered workshops are no longer allowed and work crews must involve both people with and without disabilities working together or otherwise involve workers with disabilities working with others at their worksite.
- **Develop meaningful activities in the community for those who are not working or for those who work part time.** These activities could involve volunteering, educational activities, or recreation/leisure activities out in the community that are integrated into the settings where they occur. For example, a disability agency currently takes the people in its employment development program to Habitat for Humanity and has them clean the floors as a group, not interacting with the people doing other volunteer work for the organization. This kind of "volunteering" would no longer be allowed because the people with IDD are segregated from others in this community setting. Instead, each individual would be helped to find a volunteer activity related to his or her own interests working alongside others in that organization. For example, working along with other volunteers at Habitat or another organization s/he chooses.

U.S. federal workforce development programs also changed in 2014 to encourage government funded programs to provide more services to people with disabilities and integrate them into the general workforce development system. Reauthorization of the Workforce Innovation and Opportunity Act (WIOA) stated that the American Job Centers, the one-stop-shops that provide information and referrals to federally funded job training, needed to serve people with disabilities more effectively and work more closely with the state vocational rehabilitation agencies that currently provide most employment and training

© Jo Anne Schneider 2016

services to people with disabilities. This includes co-locating voc rehab staff at American Job Centers as well as job center staff offering appropriate accommodations for people with disabilities.

WIOA also mandated that voc rehab agencies spend more of their funding on transitioning youth and start working with youth during high school in order to promote employment in the next generation of people with disabilities. While this means that much more programming is available for people early in their careers, in many states funding for older people with disabilities is more limited due to budget constraints.

More detailed information on HCBS, Employment First, and the WIOA regulations for people with disabilities is available at:

- [Medicaid website on home and community based setting rules](#)
- [Questions and answers on HCBS](#)
- [Employment first, WIOA and the HCBS final rule](#)

Taken together, these changes in societal views and legislation for people with disabilities means that more opportunities are now available for even those with the most severe disabilities to work in the community and otherwise spend their days in meaningful activities alongside other community residents. It also means that agencies need to focus on developing community based jobs and other activities that reflect the gifts, interests, and desires of each individual with a disability. New regulations also imply that agencies will need to employ more job coaches or personal assistants to support these additional people with disabilities at work, offering them sufficient training and wages to empower the person with a disability to work to their potential. Agencies will have time to transition to the new system, but individuals with disabilities and their families need

© Jo Anne Schneider 2016

to know their rights under the new regulations and be prepared to advocate for assistance finding integrated employment as envisioned by HCBS and employment first rules.

Customized Jobs and Discovery

The new HCBS rules, employment first, and WIOA together create the need for disability employment agencies to generate many more community jobs for the people they serve, and move away from simply sending people to work in the kinds of manual labor jobs traditionally held by people with disabilities unless this is the kind of work individuals want to do.

Agencies will no longer be able to say that they will only support people working during the agency's set hours, but will need to offer flexible staffing and transportation to support work. For example, an agency with set hours of 9-3 would traditionally only provide job coaches and transportation to people who worked from 10-2 so that they could be transported to and from work on the agency's vans on a set schedule during their regular hours. This agency would need to change its operations to provide transportation and support staff during the entire range of working hours, including weekends.

Leaders in employment for people with disabilities recognize that not everyone with a disability will be able to successfully compete for the full range of jobs advertised in the community. Instead, it is more effective to develop special, *customized jobs* for each individual with a disability that both meet an unmet need for the employer and genuinely use that person's gifts and interests.

The first step in developing a customized job is *discovery*. As illustrated in the last chapter, discovery involves first identifying the person's interests, followed by providing opportunities for the individual to try out those interests. In a full discovery process, agency staff would talk with many people who know the person, visit their home and do other activities to learn what they like to do. They would identify employers that could use someone with those skills and interests, often either asking for opportunities for the person to visit the workplace, volunteer, or have an internship in that setting. This allows both staff and the individual an opportunity to become clear about likes and dislikes.

A customized job is often an activity needed at the workplace, but not something that would be advertised as a full time, regular job. Staff or family members looking to create customized jobs would take into account the interests of the individual and needs of the employer, as well as whether or not the job is relatively easy to get to given available transportation options.

For example, Peter has an interest in pets, but his volunteer experiences reveal that he is interested primarily with interacting with animals, not cleaning or stocking in settings related to animals. The customized job that was eventually developed for him allowed him to fulfill the employer's need for someone to play with and feed the animals, but did not involve the full range of activities that other people at the kennel might do such as feeding the animals, giving medicine, cleaning cages, or checking pets in and out.

Developing customized jobs for people with significant disabilities involves ensuring that the employer and job coach support the person to learn the job they expect to do. If an agency offers in house opportunities for people to explore their interests, like working in a café or thrift shop for the general public operated by the agency, family and the person with a

© Jo Anne Schneider 2016

disability need to ensure that the agency sponsored business truly offers training and a launching pad for work in the community.

For example, a disability employment agency operates a cafe in a building that houses a number of organizations and offers trainings to people throughout the region. The cafe qualifies as a training site and employment venue in the community because it is in an office building used by people with and without disabilities and serves everyone in the building. While attending a training for several weeks next door to the cafe, I regularly asked for a specialty tea kept in a box on a shelf. Rather than let the person with the disability get the pack of tea, the staff person who managed the cafe insisted on getting the tea herself, even though the person with a disability clearly wanted to do it. She got angry when I encouraged her to let her employee with IDD get the tea. The employee with IDD was only allowed to run the cash register while non-disabled staff prepared all the food and got drinks for customers. While the cafe is technically offering employment and training in an integrated community setting, it does not provide its staff with the whole range of training needed to allow them to work in a similar establishment in the community.

Kevin's experience shows how important it is for families to pay attention to agency follow through on their promises to provide appropriate training and develop appropriate jobs in the community for the people they serve. In addition to his love of music, Kevin had an interest in retail and liked the idea of working in a coffee shop doing anything but running the cash register, given limited math skills. His disabilities meant that he took some time and coaching to learn a job. He was first placed in his agency's retail outlet, with the promise that he would be given training in the full range of stocking, pricing, sales, and

© Jo Anne Schneider 2016

customer service activities in the store. This was to lead to a customized job that fit his interests. But after multiple staff changes at the agency and many months watching him learn only to do back room activities at the shop like stocking and pricing, his family began to get concerned. Kevin also wondered when he would be able to get a real job. The agency provided few answers.

A new staff person with great energy started to look for customized jobs for Kevin and others at the agency. This included a visit to a music studio, but he was unable to translate that experience into either a job or volunteer experience. Instead, Kevin was offered a "volunteer job" at a local coffee shop where he was supposed to learn to prepare food and otherwise work in a restaurant. The volunteer experience offered a job coach to support him to learn his tasks. After a month learning the job, he was supposed to be offered paid work at the coffee shop.

Kevin was very proud of his job and the uniform that came with it. But after several weeks, it became clear that the untrained job coach and employer both had little interest in helping him learn to perform the tasks he expected to learn. The job coach would accompany him to the job but not do anything to help him. Sometimes she would get bored and tell him he had "done enough" and take him back to the agency after a short time. The employer only gave Kevin cleaning and table set up to do, ignoring him when he asked about learning to make sandwiches or otherwise help with food preparation. After several months of volunteering, it became clear the owner did not intend to offer a paying job.

© Jo Anne Schneider 2016

Unfortunately, Kevin's experience happens too often with many disability agencies despite their best intentions. As discussed in the chapter on working with agencies, people with disabilities and their families need to pay attention to the ability of an agency to meet employment goals. This means asking hard questions about the social capital the agency has to offer and paying attention to their training for both staff and people with disabilities they serve, expectations of employers, and staff turn over.

Even though states and the federal government both promote agencies closing down their sheltered workshops, work crews and in house employment programs that don't lead to community jobs, many agencies will only make this transition slowly and partially. Many people with disabilities and their families have expressed frustration that there are so few "good" agencies that offer quality employment programs that focus on person-centered job development reflecting the best practices described here. The agencies known for offering these services often have long waiting lists, offering few options but to try to find jobs on their own or rely on agencies using out dated employment models. This situation means that people with disabilities and their families need to advocate for customized jobs and other best practices with their agencies, reporting problems to state agencies when they occur.

The shift in policy to customized jobs in the community will mean renewed opportunities for many people with developmental disabilities with dreams of working in jobs related to their interests in the community. April is a good example of someone who has been working for pay for several years, but had to give up her dream job to do so. April is a woman with cerebral palsy and moderate intellectual disabilities that is the receptionist at her disability services agency. April

© **Jo Anne Schneider 2016**

has limited mobility due to her disabilities and has a completion certificate rather than a high school diploma. Her agency tried to help her earn a GED, but she was unable to read well enough to pass the test.

April likes her part-time job at the agency, but when I first met her she told me that she wanted to work at a day care center as a teacher or aid. While her agency supported this goal, they were unable to place her in a regular day care job because she could not take the certified training program without a high school diploma or GED and agencies were concerned that she would not be able to handle children because of her cerebral palsy. Unable to compete against people who could meet all the criteria for day care aids, April eventually gave up on her dream.

Even though she is employed in a regular job and paid wages like other employees at her agency, April's job is still a segregated job at her disability agency because she works in a setting only for people with disabilities through her employment services agency. With the new HCBS rules, her strong work history and clear ability to work with others will make her a good candidate for a customized community job. That means that her agency would be encouraged to think more creatively about helping her realize her dream of working in a day care center.

While finding work for people with significant disabilities like moderate to severe IDD is more challenging than for some others with disabilities, the same general steps are used to find work for people with a wide range of disabilities. Using social capital effectively is part of a successful discovery and customized job development process. The new U.S. federal rules and changing expectations about appropriate work for people with significant disabilities mean that people with disabilities and their families have the right to expect agencies to focus on finding community employment related to the person's

© **Jo Anne Schneider 2016**

interests. Not all agencies will successfully transition to using customized employment. Families and individuals who want these services will need to ask appropriate questions to ensure the agency can meet their expectations. Working with agencies will be discussed later in this guide. Next we look at strategies to build social capital when someone has few networks to find work.

© **Jo Anne Schneider 2016**

Building New Social Capital

Building bridging social capital for the people with disabilities can be done through several mechanisms. Identifying clubs, professional organizations, or venues to participate in activities related to the interest with others with similar interests is one key strategy. For example, Mark could develop both the cultural capital and connections to get a job working with birds of prey by joining a local club for people interested in bird rescue. Krystal could take a graduate class in counseling at a local college and develop contacts through students and teachers affiliated with the school. Sometimes, people can join virtual clubs of others with mutual interests, then meet them in person for joint activities around the interest. This can lead to developing bridging relationships. In both cases, it is important to work on developing productive connections with other members of these groups and developing appropriate cultural capital.

Joining clubs and groups is a way to develop reciprocal relationships on your own. Think about what you can contribute to these relationships. Remember, these must be reciprocal, trust based connections if they are to turn into social capital.

Fear of rejection or remembered bad experiences can serve as barriers to making contacts outside of the person with a disability's existing networks or joining clubs. If the person with a disability or family members claim that s/he can't make contacts on their own due to previous poor results or fears, it is important to remind the person that most people are kind and interested in sharing what they know. Perhaps a family member or professional working with the person with a disability can role play the bad experience or ask the person to talk it through to

© **Jo Anne Schneider 2016**

try to figure out what went wrong. Then use this negative experience to model good ways to make contact or ask for advice. Nothing is gained if you do not reach out beyond what is familiar, while moving forward can yield positive results.

It is also important to have realistic expectations of what a contact could potentially do. In most cases, the person may share some knowledge, tips, and other contacts but will have no tangible work to offer. Remember that the goal is to expand networks, not expect that networking will automatically lead to a job. Keeping expectations manageable will lead to better results.

While family members are often part of a job search using social capital, empowering people with disabilities to develop social capital and cultural capital by themselves is essential for their future. This is often a slow process that may involve many false starts. But it is essential to help the individual grow and become independent. It should be one of the goals of any job development process and is essential if a job is to become a career.

Creating Reciprocity and Long Term Relationships

I know a young man with developmental disabilities with many skills and gifts. Often, people will automatically give him things. For example, he is out walking and will go into a fast food store to use the bathroom and the staff will give him a free drink. He has learned that he can ask for things, and people will often give him something if its small, perhaps because of his disability. This is a frequent experience for some people with disabilities, even when they try to be independent.

© Jo Anne Schneider 2016

Friends, family members, and people with disabilities themselves can easily become the people that are always helped by others. Both people who know the person with disabilities well and acquaintances or strangers presume that s/he will always be on the receiving end in a social network. Or the kinds of reciprocal help people think the person with a disability can offer is limited to manual labor or being a positive presence.

It is important to get beyond this societal bias and think of people with disabilities as part of reciprocal networks. There are many ways that reciprocity can be fostered. The easiest example is helping out. For example, Peter became another volunteer at the animal shelter and Krystal volunteered at the hotline. Mark helps out at his church by handing out programs and watching children during bible school. Ryan is active at the VFW and has developed a number of contacts through his participation in this organization. All of this creates reciprocity in a network that could be called on later when looking for jobs.

Reciprocity can also be developed once a person with a disability finds a job. This could involve referring other people from their networks. Or providing advice to their company on working with disabilities. Or giving information interviews to others with disabilities.

In all cases, the person with a disability is an active member of the network, both giving and receiving. It is important to foster these mutual relationships, regardless of the nature of the disability. Everyone is capable of contributing to their networks and building long-term trusting relationships.

© Jo Anne Schneider 2016

Building Social Capital to Help Develop Careers

Often, people focus on finding people with disabilities first jobs, with some attention to maintaining employment but little thought about building a career. This is true of most employment systems for people without disabilities as well. How can people with disabilities progress in their fields and gain skills necessary to advance?

One important strategy involves identifying mentors at the workplace and elsewhere. Note that Maria served as a mentor for Krystal to help her learn how to function as a counselor. Identifying co-worker buddies and checking that these connections develop into productive relationships is an important part of ensuring someone stays at a job. Finding an older, established worker who can help an employee with a disability advance is equally important. These connections build both bridging and linking social capital for people with disabilities.

While these linking social capital connections can be found on the job, sometimes it is helpful to ensure that the person has mentors from outside of the workplace as well. Mentors found through professional organizations, clubs or other connections can both provide important advice and perspective on a first workplace, they can offer advice and connections to the next job as well.

Another important strategy involves ensuring that the person with a disability participates in professional associations or clubs affiliated with his or her interests. If the person is in an entry level job with no professional development supports, look for

© Jo Anne Schneider 2016

ways to pay for memberships and scholarships to participate in conferences.

This strategy can be used to connect people through informal clubs as well. Take Mark, the young man interested in birds. Participating in a local bird rescue society would put him in contact with people who could help him develop his interests, as well as professionals working in the field. The volunteer activities of the organization could provide both skill building and cultural capital, as well as important connections. Martin developed his career in plant biology through his experience in clubs, which later led to internships, and a career.

Mentors, professional organizations, and clubs can also provide ways to develop credentials, particularly for people that may have barriers to formal training due to disabilities. If advancing in a profession requires formal training, mentors and other connections could provide suggestions of training programs with supports and tutoring to address disabilities. Or alternative certification strategies might exist.

For all these reasons, developing initial connections for people with disabilities should involve putting in place resources needed to advance on the job. This could involve a combination of identifying mentors and facilitating memberships in professional organizations or clubs. It could be as simple as subscribing to journals or magazines affiliated with that interest that would include information on on-line forums or local clubs. In both cases, these resources build both social and cultural capital.

© Jo Anne Schneider 2016

Building Appropriate Cultural Capital

The cultural cues important to access social capital are unique to that network and vary across fields, workplaces, racial, ethnic, class and religious groups, as well as across regions and even neighborhoods. For this reason generic classes on soft skills, workplace behavior, and how to dress for the workplace only go so far in helping people with disabilities find jobs and fit in at the workplace. Appropriate cultural capital is often learned over time through experience with a network and the people in it. Friends who work in those fields are often the first and best resource, ask them to work with the individual with a disability to explain the cultural cues that are important to that network. Becoming active in clubs, internet based social networking sites, and professional associations is also an important way to develop cultural capital.

For someone who develops an interest at a young age like Martin or Mark, cultural capital development can be a gradual process. Martin first learned about the culture affiliated with plant biology through the nature center camps. Later, college courses and internship experiences built on this earlier understanding of appropriate cultural cues. By the time he was ready to find a job, he already had learned the cultural capital he would need to succeed.

For people without these early experiences, mentors or buddies that are part of the network affiliated with that interest or type of work are perhaps most effective in helping people develop appropriate cultural capital. When contacting clubs or professional associations, you can ask if anyone would be willing to serve as a guide or mentor for the person with a disability. Ask these experts in the field to share specifics of jargon,

© **Jo Anne Schneider 2016**

interaction style and other cultural attributes as well as information on the interest and potential employment. Using these mentors to develop appropriate resumes or introductory materials for job applications is also helpful as they will know what employers look for better than a generalized employment specialist.

It is also important to identify a friendly co-worker that will help a new employee learn the culture of the job. This is best done with the advice of the supervisor and explicit consent of the co-worker. As with Krystal, these buddies or mentors are important not just to learn the culture of the workplace but to progress on the job. Maria first helped Krystal understand how to dress professionally and interact with clients before referring her for information interviews for internships and jobs. This is often the case with professional jobs.

Social and cultural capital are usually built together, and it is important to pay attention to both in efforts to leverage social capital to find jobs. The positive examples throughout this guide show this process. People either learn appropriate cultural cues through their social networks, through participation in clubs, or through mentors. These are the same people that become a corner stone of their social networks.

© Jo Anne Schneider 2016

Choosing and Working with Organizations

People with disabilities can access a number of government programs and private agencies to help them find work. The resources of these organizations are part of the social capital available to people with disabilities. This chapter discusses ways to identify agencies that can best help the person with a disability find the kind of work they want to do. It outlines the kinds of social capital available through agencies and how individuals and families can encourage them to use social capital to find work. It also includes questions to ask to avoid being served by an agency that will not help meet stated employment goals.

The primary government job development organizations are state vocational rehabilitation (VR or voc rehab) agencies for people with all types of disabilities and developmental disabilities administrations for those with developmental disabilities. Most state VR organizations have a separate blind services department for people with visual disabilities and there may be special departments serving the deaf and hard or hearing. The VA also offers employment services for veterans with disabilities.

Government organizations are mandated to help people with disabilities, but they may have priorities for people with more severe disabilities or special populations. For example, Maryland's vocational rehabilitation agency, DORS (Division of Rehabilitation Services), ranks people in three categories based on the severity of their disability and several other factors. People in category one (more severe disabilities) and transitioning youth are generally served soon after they apply. People in category two (moderate disabilities) may be on a waiting list that could be six months to several years. Given

© Jo Anne Schneider 2016

limited funding, category three cases may never be served. People who receive comprehensive employment services from state developmental disabilities administrations may need to prove that they need help with three of five categories of daily living to get support.

Explore the benefits available through these organizations in high school for people with disabilities acquired as children and soon after the disability for adults. It is important to understand the criteria for service and the types of services provided by these organizations before you need them. States, school districts, and organizations for people with disabilities often have information and advice on these services. If you are eligible, it is often a good idea to apply.

Centers for Independent Living (CIL), which are nonprofits created through federal law and which receive some government funding, are also an excellent resource for advice on government and private programs. CILs are located throughout the country and there is also a state umbrella group for its CILS that can provide a list of CILs serving your area. Part of their government mandate is to provide information and referrals to people with disabilities. Some also offer employment services.

Government agencies can provide assessments, direct services, and referral to training and private organizations that provide service for free or on a sliding scale, depending on the person with a disability's resources. They often refer people to private organizations to provide employment services.

Beyond these government agencies, there are a wide array of non-profit and for-profit organizations and individual counselors that help people with disabilities find jobs. Families and people with disabilities can either access these agencies for free through a government referral or pay for services themselves.

© **Jo Anne Schneider 2016**

The organizations vary greatly and picking the right one can involve a lot of research.

In some cases, your social capital networks can help you with that. Ask friends or people you know from disability associated organizations about their experience with employment organizations. For example, Ryan could ask people he knew from the VFW about their experience with employment agencies for disabled vets. Parents with youth in Special Olympics can ask other families and individuals participating in the program about their experience. Resource coordinators (sometimes called service coordinators or coordinators of community services), who are provided by the state to give advice to people with developmental disabilities and their families about available services, can also provide this kind of referral information if they are experienced.

Like the Jewish employment agency that helped Marion find work, organization often rely on their own social capital to find jobs for the people they serve. The next section looks at organizational social capital.

Organizational Social Capital

Organizations have social capital in their own right, as organizations. Organizational social capital is more than just the sum total of the social capital of its staff and board, but comes from the relationships the organization has established over time. Organizations also have networks of funders, government agencies, and other organizations that support their work that can also be put to work to help find jobs for their participants.

Organizational social capital comes from two places: 1) the established reputation of the organization and 2) social capital through relationships with other organizations that the agency

© Jo Anne Schneider 2016

has developed over time. The same can be true for any organization that is visible in a community over time. An organization can foster this kind of social capital by participating actively in community events or organizations like the Chamber of Commerce or service organizations like Rotary.

Partnerships to provide services can also create these kinds of social capital networks. For example, regularly developed volunteer activities like social activities in nursing homes, volunteering in soup kitchens, or fostering boy and girl scout troops that include people with disabilities and encourage adults with disabilities at the agency to serve as assistant scoutmasters can build these relationships. In cases like a soup kitchen, Habitat for Humanity or other organizations that draw volunteers from many organizations, this can build relationships with both the organization offering the service and the churches, scout troops, or other organizations that are also sources of volunteers.

These organizations not only provide potential places that individuals with disabilities can find work, their staff and participants can serve as bridging or linking connections for people with disabilities. For instance, a scout master may work as an HR representative in an agency looking for someone to serve as a facilitator and advocate for people with disabilities in a large company. If your counselor was connected to this scout master, she may be able to help someone like Selma find a job. The head of volunteers at a soup kitchen might reveal that the volunteer liaison for a church that provides meals at a homeless shelter where the disability agency also sends volunteers regularly is the falcon expert at a bird sanctuary, providing an important connection for Mark.

© Jo Anne Schneider 2016

An often overlooked organizational social capital network for disability services agencies is their suppliers, organizations providing professional services, and their sponsors or funders. Accounting firms, IT service companies, web designers, printers, food and office supply companies, clinics providing medical services, payroll or billing services, have established relationships that can be used as networks for people served by the agency. Likewise, foundations and government agencies funding programs have a vested interest in their success. Agency staff could turn to these organizations to provide internships or contacts into other networks that fit the interests of people with disabilities served by the agency.

Using the organization's networks can yield an expanded array of organizations doing multiple types of work. By carefully cultivating these partners as resources for people served by the agency, these organizations are more likely to welcome program participants or provide them with advice. Organizational networks also can educate employees on what is required to find appropriate work for someone served by their agency. For instance, an IT firm might identify a number of different ways someone facile with a computer could find work that an employment specialist may not know about. Expanding information and contacts should be an ongoing part of staff development as well as finding individualized employment for people with disabilities.

In working with an agency, you might ask if they are using these types of contacts to find work for the people they serve. If they aren't, you may need to ask how this kind of networking can be developed. Ask them about internships and how the other programs of the agency might provide contacts or internship opportunities related to the person with disability's interest.

© **Jo Anne Schneider 2016**

The point is to ensure the agency is using the networks it has available to help find appropriate work.

In addition to the social capital inherent in an organization, organization staff and board also have social networks that could be activated for people served by the agency. This is more delicate, as staff may not want to merge work and their private life. But if the counselor is willing to use personal contacts, this may expand the network available to the person with a disability. Show them your social capital list and ask if they could develop their own to help the person with a disability find work.

A Word on Job Clubs

Job clubs are a tool that employment agencies often use to help people finding work. A job club is a group of people looking for work. They may be a group of people in the same field, or just people placed with the same agency. The idea is that people will develop networks with the people in their club and share leads or contacts. In this way, job club members can share social capital and help each other find jobs.

In some cases, job clubs can be effective ways to help people find work. However, bringing together a group of unemployed people may lead nowhere as none of them may have contacts that lead to work. Or, as with Krystal, those networks may not have the connections to find an appropriate job.

Job clubs may be an important source of other resources, moral support, and potential leads. As such, they should not be avoided altogether. But if your agency wants you to participate in a job club, find out why and what resources they think the job

© **Jo Anne Schneider 2016**

club could offer. It is important to know that the organization is using other types of social capital resources like organizational or staff contacts rather than relying on job clubs as the major source of social capital.

Things to Look for in Choosing an Agency

When working with someone in an agency, think of them as someone who has access to networks to jobs through both their personal networks and the organization. You want to make sure that the organization has the kinds of connections that will help find the person with a disability the kind of job they want, not just any job. You also want to be sure that the organization shares the same philosophy about work and the person with disability that you do. In other words, is their cultural capital compatible with your goals? In order to determine if an organization has the right social and cultural capital, it is often helpful to find answers to the following questions:

1. Does this organization have a track record of finding jobs similar to the type of work the person with a disability wants to do?
2. Do they have a philosophy of developing customized jobs and a proven track record of creating work related to a person's interests?
3. If the person is a professional or aspires to a profession or skilled trade, do the support finding work in a person's field and related to their training? Do they have the resources to place professionals in professional jobs? Do they have a track record of doing this?
4. Does the agency work with family or individual with disability networks and use their own networks to find appropriate work?

© Jo Anne Schneider 2016

5. Does the culture, philosophy, and service strategy of the agency fit with the person with the disability's expectations and goals?

Families and individuals need to use the answers to these questions to identify organizations that can productively help in the job search. While families and individuals can seldom choose their counselor at VR, developmental disabilities, or a department of veteran's affairs, they can ask for counselors that specialize in a certain kind of jobs or share a particular view of people with disabilities. A productive match with a government counselor is often essential to using government to achieve employment goals.

Ensuring that a government or private agency knows what social capital really means and is willing to use it as a tool to help in a job search is part of the initial research you will want to do when choosing an agency. While an important tool, using social capital is most effective if combined with other employment tools that agencies use to place people in jobs. It is not the only way that people find jobs. You will want to ask about the range of services, strategies, and supports the organization has to help in the job search.

Individuals with disabilities and families should go into VR or the developmental disabilities agency with a list of agencies they want to work with. It is important to have done this homework ahead of time and to lobby for referrals to agencies that you feel comfortable with and have a track record in finding the kind of work the person with a disability wants. This is the best way to leverage the resources of government and private entities. Once referred to a private organization, you may ask about the staff and ask if you can be referred to staff who have a reputation for helping find the kinds of jobs the person with a

© **Jo Anne Schneider 2016**

disability wants. You can ask to change counselors or employment specialists. You are looking for someone with a similar philosophy and who appears to have the resources and vision to find jobs that fit the interest of the person with a disability.

In some cases, you may be relying on the social capital of a particular job developer or employment specialist. The person may use their personal networks to help the person with a disability find work. But in most cases, they will be using resources available through the organization.

If you have a specific kind of work in mind, you do need to know if the counselor understands this kind of work and if they can refer the person with a disability to people who can help him find work connected to that interest or field. You may want to ask if they use social networks to help find jobs. You should encourage them to ask about your networks and involve you actively in the job search.

© Jo Anne Schneider 2016

Tips for Effectively Using Social Capital in Employment for People with Disabilities

This chapter summarizes some key strategies to help people with disabilities and their families use social capital effectively to find work.

- **Social capital means *the social relationships and patterns of reciprocal, enforceable trust that enable people and institutions to gain access to resources like social services, jobs, or government contracts.*** People in a network look for appropriate cultural capital when deciding whether or not they want to share their resources. Successfully using social capital involves identifying three ingredients: connections, reciprocal trust, and cultural capital. Individuals and families should ask these questions when identifying useful connections:

    1. Does anyone in the individual's personal networks either work in the field where s/he has an interest or work in a place that is related to that interest?
    2. Does that person have useful connections to places or people that could lead to a paying job related to that interest?
    3. Is that person willing to use those connections to help the person with a disability find work in that field?

- **Social capital networks useful to help individuals find work can be found in the personal networks of the person with disabilities, through clubs and professional organizations, and through government and private agencies that provide employment services.** People with disabilities should be

© Jo Anne Schneider 2016

prepared to seek appropriate connections through all of these sources.

- **Helping people learn appropriate cultural capital for a field or workplace is equally important if they are going to effectively use social capital connections and succeed at a job.** Cultural capital is specific to a particular kind of work or workplace. Those helping a person with a disability find work need to be careful to recognize cultural cues relevant for a target type of work or employer. Some strategies to achieve this include:
    - Asking the person serving as the social capital link to a job to help develop resumes or job presentation materials for someone seeking a job in that field.
    - Asking the social capital link or a mentor to help the person learn the culture of the workplace or field.
    - Paying attention to the ways that people dress and act when visiting employers.
    - Encouraging people with disabilities to identify and participate in clubs, online forums, or professional associations affiliated with their interests and asking them to pay attention to the language, dress and other aspects of the culture of that field.

- **Bonding, Bridging, and Linking social capital are equally important and should be identified and built for individuals with disabilities.**
    - Bonding networks include people most familiar with the person with the disability, but it is important to determine if they have the resources needed to find work in the targeted field.
    - Bridging networks may exist through the individual's bonding networks or those of staff at a disability

© **Jo Anne Schneider 2016**

employment organization. Look for bridging individuals or clubs or online forums that can facilitate building bridging connections. Remember that bridging connections also rely on enforceable trust and will not be created by sending someone to a career fair or one visit to a club.
  - Linking social capital involves individuals or organizations with a reciprocal relationship that is unequal. Identify linking social capital in a person with disability's networks or creating linking resources through mentors.

- **Mentors are an important resource, but the mentor needs to have access to resources that can help the person with a disability find a job and be willing to share those connections.** Mentors are also a key resource to learn appropriate cultural capital and should be asked specifically to facilitate learning the culture of the workplace and field.

- **Clubs, online forums, post-secondary education courses, and professional organizations can serve as places where people with disabilities can develop bridging and linking social capital for jobs related to their interests.** These groups can also be places to develop appropriate cultural capital.

- **Developing workplace buddies and mentors through relationships with co-workers is important both to succeed on the job and move up.** Co-workers placed in buddy or mentor roles should be willing participants with the goal to help the person with a disability learn the workplace culture and develop connections.

© Jo Anne Schneider 2016

- **People with disabilities and their families would do well to familiarize themselves with recent policy changes impacting on available services and be prepared to advocate for best practices outlined in these policies.** Recent changes in public policy mandate that agencies serving people with disabilities make every effort to develop meaningful activities and employment in the community based on the person's interests and goals, regardless of the nature or severity of their disability. Policy also emphasizes finding work for people with disabilities in the community. Government resources designed for the general public also are required to do a better job of accommodating people with disabilities.

- **Government agencies and disability job development or employment programs may have additional social capital that can help in the job search.** But you need to make sure they understand what social capital is, have compatible cultural capital, and are willing to work with you to use social capital to find work for the person with a disability. Individuals and families need to do research with organizations and interview them regarding the social capital they have available and their track record of using it to help people with disabilities find work before signing on with an agency or program.

© Jo Anne Schneider 2016

Appendix: The Theory and Research Behind Social Capital

While social capital was popularized by Robert Putnam, the concept was developed much earlier and has been used in several ways. Three major scholars are generally credited with developing social capital: Robert Putnam (1995, 2000, Putnam and Feldstein 2003) in Political Science, James Coleman (1988) in Sociology, and Pierre Bourdieu (1984, 1986 and Bourdieu and Wacquant 1992) in Philosophy and Anthropology. Alejandro Portes (Portes 1998, Portes and Landolt 1996, Portes and Sensenbrenner 1993), an Economic Sociologist, has also played a significant role in developing Coleman and Bourdieu's concepts.

Scholars at the World Bank, particularly Woolcock and Narayan (World Bank 2001, Woolcock 1998, Woolcock and Narayan 2000), have also played a significant role in furthering the concept as it applies to development as well as developing the concept of linking social capital. Linking social capital has also been adopted as an important way to understand patron/client relationships in the U.S. and other parts of the developed world.

These key thinkers' works have evolved into two camps. Proponents of Putnam's version of social capital, known through the work of the Saguaro seminar, focus on the role of social capital in civic engagement and as a community wide indicator of civic health. Civic engagement refers to participation in activities meant to increase the public good like volunteering, contributing to the United Way, or voting. Putnam defines social capital as "social networks, norms of reciprocity, mutual assistance and trustworthiness" (Putnam and Feldstein 2003: 2). This approach is used by scholars interested in community wide

© Jo Anne Schneider 2016

civic engagement and social capital is seen as generated through fact to face interactions in organizations that foster trust in the community. Since Putnam's works have been popularized in the United States and elsewhere, he is often named as the source for social capital as a concept.

The strategies people with disabilities and their families hope to use to increase employment for people with disabilities are more closely linked to the research of social scientists who study social capital and social networks. Social scientists interested in the role of social capital in opportunity, social equity, poverty and development draw on Coleman (1988), Bourdieu (1986) and Portes (1998) work to explore the role of trust based social networks and cultural capital in opportunity structures for various populations. This research draws on earlier social network theory for individuals (Stack 1974, Granovetter 1973 and 1985, Burt 1992).

Coleman looked at face to face trust based networks that supported schools. Carol Stack showed how poor families rely on the resources of their social networks, but that the limits of those networks can hold them back. Grannoveter showed the importance or bridging ties to get into new networks while Burt spent his career exploring how social capital shapes careers. Portes has looked at social capital for marginalized groups like immigrants, showing how the connections people form in this country and the culture of both their bonding groups of other immigrants and the community where they are resettled influence life chances.

French scholar Bourdieu was interested in how societies maintained differences between groups, particularly those of different classes. Social capital was one of three types of capital:

© Jo Anne Schneider 2016

social, economic and cultural capital. While all definitions of social capital acknowledge that norms or culture are central to functioning networks, Bourdieu showed the real importance of cultural capital in defining who could access resources of a particular network.

The differences between Putnam and this social science school stems as much from the different problems they explore as different understandings of theory. While Putnam and followers focus primarily on the role of social capital in promoting community wide civic health, Portes and others from the social sciences focus primarily on the impact of social capital for individuals or marginalized communities. The World Bank initiative focused on the role of social capital in alleviating poverty (World Bank 2001) has begun to develop a middle ground between these two approaches by focusing on both institutions involved in community wide development and the impact of social capital for individuals attempting to gain access to community wide resources.

The definitions used in this guide come primarily from the social science school, with acknowledgement of Putnam's later contributions in bridging social capital. Theoretically, I draw primarily on Portes and Bourdieu. Readers interested in more detailed discussion of social capital as a concept and its use here will find more detailed discussion in *Social Capital and Welfare Reform* (Schneider 2006) and *Organizational Social Capital and Nonprofits* (Schneider 2009).

© **Jo Anne Schneider 2016**

References

Bourdieu, Pierre. (1984) *Distinction*. Richard Nice (transl). Cambridge, MA: Harvard University Press.
---(1986) The Forms of Capital. In *Handbook of Theory and Research for the Sociology of Education*. John G. Richardson (editor). Richard Nice (Transl). New York: Greenwood Press.

Bourdieu, Pierre and Loic J.D. Wacquant (1992) *An Invitation to Reflexive* Sociology. Chicago: University of Chicago Press.

Burt, R (1992) *Structural Holes: The Social Structure of Competition.* Boston: Harvard University Press.

Coleman, James. (1988) Social Capital in the Creation of Human Capital. *American Journal of Sociology,* 94 Supplement: S95-S120.

Fernandez Kelly, Patricia (1995) Social and Cultural Capital in the Urban Ghetto: Implications for the Economic Sociology of Immigration. In *The Economic Sociology of Immigration: Essays on Networks, Ethnicity and Entrepreneurship.* Alejandro Portes, editor. New York: Russell Sage Foundation: 213-247.

Granovetter, Mark. (1973) The Strength of Weak Ties. *American Journal of Sociology,* 78 (6): 1360-1380.

--(1985). Economic Action and Social Structure: The Problem of Embededdedness. *American Journal of Sociology* 91 (3): 481-510.

Portes, Alejandro (1998) Social Capital: Its Origins and Applications in Modern Sociology. *Annual Review of Sociology*: 1-24.

© **Jo Anne Schneider 2016**

Portes, Alejandro and Patricia Landolt (1996) The Downside of Social Capital. *The American Prospect,* 26: 18-21.

Portes, Alejandro and Sensenbrenner, Julia. (1993) Embeddedness and Immigration: Notes on the Social Determinants of Economic Action. *American Journal of Sociology*, 98(6): 1320-1350.

Putnam, Robert.(1995) Bowling Alone: America's Declining Social Capital. *Journal of Democracy,* 6(1): 65-78.
--(2000) *Bowling Alone: The Collapse and Revival of American Community.* New York: Simon and Schuster.

Putnam, Robert and Lewis Feldstein (2003). *Better Together: Restoring the American Community.* New York: Simon and Schuster.

Schneider, Jo Anne (2006) *Social Capital and Welfare Reform.* New York: Columbia University Press.
--(2009). Organizational social capital and nonprofits. In M.E. Harris (Guest Editor), Nonprofits and voluntary action: Theories and concepts. *Nonprofit and Voluntary Sector Quarterly*, 38(4), 643-662.

Stack, Carol (1974) *All Our Kin: Strategies for Survival in a Black Community.* New York: Harper and Row.

Woolcock, Michael (1998) Social Capital and Economic Development: Toward a Theoretical Synthesis and Policy Framework. *Theory and Society* 22: 151-208.

Woolcock, Michael and Deepap Narayan (2000) Social Capital: Implications for Development Theory, Research and Policy. *World Bank Research Observer,* 15 (2): 225-249.

World Bank (2001). *World development report 2000/2001: Attacking poverty.* New York: Oxford University Press.

© Jo Anne Schneider 2016

Related Publications

In this Series

Using Social Capital to get Jobs for People with Disabilities: A Primer for Agencies

Other Key Publications by Jo Anne Schneider on Social Capital (see http://chrysaliscollaborations.com/publications-workshops-webinars/ for links)

Schneider, J.A. (2010). Social capital and social geography. Annie E. Casey Foundation. Baltimore: Annie E. Casey Foundation.

Schneider, J.A. (2009). Organizational social capital and nonprofits. In M.E. Harris (Guest Editor), Nonprofits and voluntary action: Theories and concepts. *Nonprofit and Voluntary Sector Quarterly*, 38(4), 643-662.

Schneider, J.A. (2007). Connections and disconnections between civic engagement and social capital in community based non-profits. Nonprofit and Voluntary Sector Quarterly, December 2007, volume 36(4), 572-597

Schneider, J.A. (2006). Small nonprofits and civil society: Civic engagement and social capital. In R.A. Cnaan, & C. Milofsky (Eds.), *Handbook of community movements and local organizations.* 74-88. New York: Springer.

Schneider, J.A. (2006). *Social capital and welfare reform: Organizations, congregations and communities.* New York: Columbia University Press.

© **Jo Anne Schneider 2016**

Schneider, J.A. (2005). Getting beyond the training vs. work experience debate: the role of labor markets, social capital, cultural capital, and community resources in long term poverty. In H. Hartmann (Guest Editor), Women, work and poverty: Women centered research in policy change. *Women, Politics, and Policy,* 27(3/4), 41-54.

Schneider, J.A. (2004). *The role of social capital in building healthy communities.* Baltimore, MD: Annie E. Casey Foundation.

Schneider, J.A. (2003). Small minority based non-profits in the information age: Examples from Kenosha, WI. **Nonprofit Management and Leadership,** 13(4), 383-399.

Schneider, J.A. (2002). Social capital and community supports for low income families: Examples from Pennsylvania and Wisconsin. Social Policy Journal. 1(1), 35-56.

Schneider, J.A. (2001). Kenosha Social Capital Project education report: Churches, non-profits and community. Indiana, PA: Indiana University of Pennsylvania.

Schneider, J.A. (2000). Pathways to opportunity: The role of race, social networks, institutions and neighborhood in career and educational paths for people on welfare. Human Organization, 59(1), 72-85.

© **Jo Anne Schneider 2016**

www.ingramcontent.com/pod-product-compliance
Lightning Source LLC
Chambersburg PA
CBHW061157180526
45170CB00002B/839